S0-FDE-894

Kansas City, MO Public Library
0000189188444

ROURKE'S SCHOOL to HOME CONNECTIONS
BEFORE AND DURING READING ACTIVITIES

Before Reading: *Building Background Knowledge and Vocabulary*

Building background knowledge can help children process new information and build upon what they already know. Before reading a book, it is important to tap into what children already know about the topic. This will help them develop their vocabulary and increase their reading comprehension.

Questions and Activities to Build Background Knowledge:

1. Look at the front cover of the book and read the title. What do you think this book will be about?
2. What do you already know about this topic?
3. Take a book walk and skim the pages. Look at the table of contents, photographs, captions, and bold words. Did these text features give you any information or predictions about what you will read in this book?

Vocabulary: *Vocabulary Is Key to Reading Comprehension*

Use the following directions to prompt a conversation about each word.

- Read the vocabulary words.
- What comes to mind when you see each word?
- What do you think each word means?

Vocabulary Words:
- activist
- drag
- gender
- LGBTQ
- movement
- pride
- protested
- uprising

During Reading: *Reading for Meaning and Understanding*

To achieve deep comprehension of a book, children are encouraged to use close reading strategies. During reading, it is important to have children stop and make connections. These connections result in deeper analysis and understanding of a book.

 Close Reading a Text

During reading, have children stop and talk about the following:

- Any confusing parts
- Any unknown words
- Text to text, text to self, text to world connections
- The main idea in each chapter or heading

Encourage children to use context clues to determine the meaning of any unknown words. These strategies will help children learn to analyze the text more thoroughly as they read.

When you are finished reading this book, turn to the next-to-last page for **Text-Dependent Questions** and an **Extension Activity**.

TABLE OF CONTENTS

TAKING ACTION

Have you ever stood up to another person? Someone who wished you would just stay quiet? Sylvia Rivera was probably scared to stand up—but she was also very brave.

LIBERATION

POLICE LINE

The night was dark. Sirens blared. People were getting hurt and arrested just because they were members of the **LGBTQ** community. Sylvia knew it wasn't right. She was going to tell her truth. She wouldn't stay quiet! Sylvia was an **activist** who took action to make the world a better place.

RISING UP

Sylvia Rivera was born in 1951 in New York City. Her parents were Puerto Rican and Venezuelan. As a child, Sylvia was raised by her grandmother. When she was born, Sylvia was labeled as a boy. But from a very young age, she knew that label was wrong.

Sylvia used makeup and clothes to express herself. She loved to dress up. Kids at school didn't like this. They bullied her and even beat her up. At times, school was a scary place for Sylvia. Around the age of 11, she ran away from home.

After she ran away, Sylvia didn't live in just one place. She moved around during her teenage years. Sometimes she lived in buildings or in tents. It was a difficult way to live.

In 1963, Sylvia met a friend who would change her life. Her name was Marsha P. Johnson. Marsha was a **drag** queen and an activist. Marsha and other drag queens taught Sylvia that it was okay to wear makeup and dresses. Sylvia could express her **gender** however she liked.

Sylvia was learning that it was okay to be herself. In fact, it was great.

Sylvia spent more and more time with Marsha and the other drag queens. Soon, Sylvia became an activist too. She wanted to stand up for other LGBTQ people.

On June 28, 1969, she got her chance. That night, there was an **uprising** at the Stonewall Inn in New York City. The police were kicking people out of the Stonewall Inn. They were arresting some of the drag queens and LGBTQ people. So, they decided to fight back.

13

LGBTQ people needed a place where they could express themselves without fear. They needed to feel safe. That night, they raised their voices and their fists.

Sylvia stood up...

...she raised her voice...

...she wouldn't back down.

For six days and nights, the activists **protested**. They were not going to back down, no matter what.

LEAVING A LEGACY

Stonewall was just the beginning. Those protests helped spark the modern LGBTQ rights **movement**. After Stonewall, more and more LGBTQ people began to come out.

In the months after Stonewall, Sylvia helped lead even more protests. In the 1970s, the first **pride** parades were held. Sylvia and other transgender people were discouraged from attending. Some people didn't accept them as part of the LGBTQ community.

Sylvia knew that the LGBTQ community was big enough for everyone. At one pride parade in 1973, she grabbed the microphone. She spoke out for drag queens and transgender people. When Sylvia raised her voice, people listened.

STAR

Sylvia and Marsha started a group to support and house transgender women and youth. The STAR House was a safe space for those in the LGBTQ community. Sylvia called the youth at the STAR House her kids.

In 2002, Sylvia passed away, but her story lives on. Today, lawyers at the Sylvia Rivera Law Project help LGBTQ people like Sylvia. They fight for their safety and rights. Sylvia showed the world just how powerful one person can be. We can stand up, speak out. If enough individuals do this... together, we can change the world.

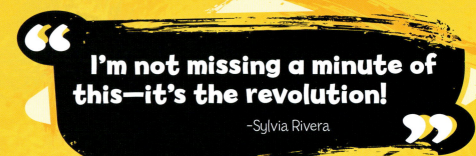

" I'm not missing a minute of this—it's the revolution! "

-Sylvia Rivera

TIME LINE

1951   Sylvia Rivera is born.

1962   Sylvia leaves home at the age of 11.

1963   Marsha P. Johnson and Sylvia Rivera meet for the first time.

1969   The Stonewall Uprising in New York City ignites the movement for LGBTQ rights.

1970   The first official Pride Parade is held in New York City.

1992   Marsha P. Johnson, Sylvia's best friend, passes away in New York City.

1993   Sylvia moves into a house like the STAR House, where she can find support. There, she regains her health.

1994   Sylvia is honored at a march marking the 25th anniversary of the Stonewall Uprising.

2002   Sylvia passes away from liver cancer.

2002   The Sylvia Rivera Law Project, a legal aid organization dedicated to helping transgender, intersex, and gender non-conforming people, opens in New York City.

2005   The corner of Christopher and Hudson streets in New York City was renamed "Sylvia Rivera Way."

2015   A portrait of Sylvia is added to the National Portrait Gallery in Washington, DC, making her the first-ever transgender activist to be included in the museum.

GLOSSARY

activist (AK-tiv-ist): a person who takes action in support of, or in opposition to, a controversial issue

drag (drag): a type of entertainment in which performers challenge gender stereotypes, typically by exaggerating stereotypes from another gender, such as dressing up in elaborate clothing or using gendered mannerisms

gender (JEN-dur): the traits, such as behavioral or cultural, that are typically associated with one sex

LGBTQ (ell-gee-bee-tee-kyoo): lesbian, gay, bisexual, transgender, and queer/questioning

movement (MOOV-muhnt): a group of people working together to promote a cause

pride (pride): a sense of one's own importance or worth, adopted by the LGBTQ community to assert their right to exist without shame

protested (PROH-test-id): to have demonstrated or stood up against something

uprising (UHP-rye-zing): a revolt or rebellion

INDEX

TEXT-DEPENDENT QUESTIONS

1. Who was Sylvia's best friend?
2. When did Sylvia run away from home?
3. Where did Sylvia live at the end of her life?
4. Why did the Stonewall uprising happen?
5. How did kids at school react to Sylvia?

EXTENSION ACTIVITY

Sylvia Rivera was one of many activists who spoke out for LGBTQ rights. At protests, activists often speak up through signs, songs, and dances—even ginormous puppets or impressive parade floats! Now's your chance to let your voice be heard. Think about an issue that matters to you. Then, design your own sign that expresses how you feel. Have an adult help you make a stick to hold the sign up. The next time people gather for a peaceful protest, you'll be ready to raise your sign and your voice— just like Sylvia.

ABOUT THE AUTHOR

Kaitlyn Duling knows that words have the power to change lives. Kaitlyn grew up in Illinois, but now lives with her wife in Washington, DC. There are protests, rallies, and marches in DC almost every single day! Kaitlyn has written more than 100 books for children and teens. She hopes her books will inspire readers to stand up and speak out in the face of injustice.

ABOUT THE ILLUSTRATOR

David Wilkerson was born in Denver, CO and is currently based in Maryland. He developed a love for illustration during his high school years. His career began in the animation industry, working as a character designer, prop designer, and background designer. He has worked as a designer on projects for: Hulu, Cartoon Network, Springhill Company, FOX Sports, and FUSE. He believes that there is healing in storytelling, and that it is the job of creatives to contribute to that cause.

© 2023 Rourke Educational Media

All rights reserved. No part of this book may be reproduced or utilized in any form or by any means, electronic or mechanical including photocopying, recording, or by any information storage and retrieval system without permission in writing from the publisher.

www.rourkebooks.com

PHOTO CREDITS: page 20: ©Harvey Wang-2021

Quote source: Emma Rothberg. "Sylvia Rivera." National Women's History Museum, March 2021: https://www.womenshistory.org/education-resources/biographies/sylvia-rivera

Edited by: Hailey Scragg
Illustrations by: David Wilkerson
Cover and interior layout by: J.J. Giddings

Library of Congress PCN Data

Sylvia Rivera / Kaitlyn Duling
(Leaders Like Us)
ISBN 978-1-73165-282-9 (hard cover)
ISBN 978-1-73165-252-2 (soft cover)
ISBN 978-1-73165-312-3 (e-book)
ISBN 978-1-73165-342-0 (e-pub)
Library of Congress Control Number: 2021952186

Rourke Educational Media
Printed in the United States of America
01-2412211937